Locke

IN 90 MINUTES

Paul Strathern

IVAN R. DEE
CHICAGO

Library of Congress Cataloging-in-Publication Data:
Strathern, Paul, 1940–

    Locke in 90 minutes / Paul Strathern
      p.   cm. — (Philosophers in 90 minutes)
    Includes bibliographical references and index.
    ISBN 1-56663-261-7 (alk. paper). — ISBN 1-56663-262-5
(pbk. : alk. paper)
    1. Locke, John, 1632–1704. I. Title. II. Series.
B1296.S77 1999
192—dc21   99-34484

Contents

LOCKE IN 90 MINUTES

Introduction

Philosophy moves backward. It began with an infinite universe of complex, beautiful, and often conflicting ideas. Gradually, with the aid of religious bigotry, reason, and the will to understand, philosophy began to shrink this world to more comprehensible proportions. Everything became simpler, more obvious. Philosophy was regressing to the point where it described the world as we actually see it. With John Locke philosophy enters its flat-earth period.

Great ideas are often obvious. None more so than those of John Locke. Much of his thought we would now regard as common sense. His philosophy was to lay the foundations of empiricism, with its belief that our knowledge of the world is based on experience. It also introduced the idea of liberal democracy, which has become the shibboleth of Western civilization. People who can't even spell *philosophy* are now likely to accept these philosophical tenets, which were incomprehensible just over three centuries ago.

This all makes Locke's philosophy rather uninteresting. But there's no reason why philosophy shouldn't be dull. On the contrary, there are very good reasons why it *should* be dull. It was when works of philosophy became interesting, and people actually began reading them, that the trouble started. People who read things are liable to believe in them, and then look what happens. The earlier part of the twentieth century remains as a hideous reminder of what happens when large groups of people start taking philosophy seriously. Fortunately, philosophy has now progressed well beyond the infantile stage where people who read it are expected to believe in it. But this was not always the case—and many of the wisest philosophers have realized the pitfall of readers actually understanding what they were saying. Spinoza did his best to solve this problem by rendering his works unreadable. Socrates, on the other hand, decided that the best way was not to write down anything at all. (The former tactic was adopted by philosophers such as Kant and Hegel, the latter by Polique, Ehrensvard, and Huntingdon-Jones.) Locke's solution was to write philosophy that was so obvious it soon appeared dull. But it wasn't always so. Locke's thought and ideas were revolutionary in their time and altered the course of philosophy.

Locke was the only major philosopher to become a government minister. And it shows. He was a man of many parts, but he remained for the most part consistent and practical. His philosophy is one that actually works—for both the individual and society at large.

Locke's Life and Works

Locke attempted to live a life that was almost as dull as his philosophy. Fortunately for us, though not for him, he lived in exciting times—and couldn't avoid getting involved. John Locke was born on August 29, 1632, in a small, rather grubby thatched cottage by the church in the Somerset village of Wrington. His father was an unambitious country lawyer and his mother a tanner's daughter, who was reputed to have been a great beauty. Soon after John's birth his parents moved to a family property near the small market town of Pensford, just south of Bristol. Here Locke grew up in a Tudor farmhouse called Belluton. This building has long since disappeared, but the house that now occupies the site is said to have been built on its foundations. It stands on a hill above the rather ordinary little town of Pensford, but here on a summer's day you have a breathtaking view out over the Mendip Hills in the direction of Midsommer Norton and Downside Abbey.

This rural idyll was shattered by the outbreak of the civil war in 1642, when John was ten. The war was the culmination of a long-standing dispute between King Charles I and Parliament. Charles believed in the divine right of kings, according to which the monarch received his authority direct from God, and was thus not answerable to institutions run by mere mortals, such as Parliament. The members of Parliament, who were responsible for voting the king his cash, thought otherwise. In fact, the civil war was basically a stand-up fight between the emerging merchantile class in the red corner, with the king and his landed aristocracy in the blue corner. It tore the country apart and was to bring about the first successful revolution in European history.

The Locke family supported the Parliamentarians. The local member of Parliament, Alexander Popham, became colonel of the regional Parliamentary militia and appointed Locke's father as his captain. Locke's father left home to join the campaign. After coming across a few unsuspecting Royalist columns, which they quickly put to flight, Colonel Popham's militia joined up with the Parliamentary army at Devizes. But this time the Royalists were prepared, and in the ensuing rout Locke's father and Popham were lucky to escape with their lives. After this they "decided to withdraw from the military life" and returned home.

By now the country was in turmoil, and Locke's family found themselves without means of support. Colonel Popham did his best for his old captain but only managed to secure him a post as the country clerk for sewers (this may well reflect how both these ex-warriors were held in local esteem).

In 1646 Charles I was captured, and three years later he was beheaded. The Commonwealth was established, with Oliver Cromwell soon emerging as its head. Meanwhile Colonel Popham was able to do a further favor for his friend Captain Locke. As a member of Parliament he was allowed to nominate pupils for entry to Westminster School in London, the finest in the land at the time. This favor, which he granted to the son of an obscure impecunious west-country lawyer, was to change John Locke's life. Without such an education it is doubtful whether Locke would have had the opportunity to realize his exceptional talents.

Curiously, although Westminster was controlled by a Parliamentary committee, it retained a Royalist headmaster. This was a failed actor called Dr. Busby, renowned for his dramatic and sadistic floggings. According to the poet John Dryden, who was a contemporary of Locke's at Westminster, "our Master Busby used to whip a boy so long, till he made him a confirmed blockhead." But the essayist Richard Steele, who was also a pupil, was of the opinion that Busby had "a genius for education." And, astonishingly, this is the view that has prevailed. Two centuries later the prime minister William Gladstone commended Dr. Busby as "the founder of the public school system."

John Locke was a frail youngster, and the prospect of an encounter with Dr. Busby doubtless stimulated his dormant intellectual faculties to the full. As one of the brightest scholars at Westminster, Locke would certainly have got to know the precocious Dryden, who was already publishing poetry before he left school. Dryden appears to have learned something from his Royalist headmaster's survival technique—in a school that stood in the very shadow of Parliament, during a time when the king was executed just across Parliament Square in Whitehall. At the age of twenty-six Dryden was to write a heroic tribute to Oliver Cromwell. Two years later, when the monarchy was restored, Dryden composed an equally mellifluous celebration of Charles II, and was later rewarded with the post of poet laureate. While poet laureate he composed a paean to the Anglican church; but when the Catholic James II ascended to the throne he changed his mind, became a Roman Catholic, and wrote an epic celebration of Catholicism.

Unfortunately this time he was caught, because a few years later the Protestant King William assumed the throne, and Dryden was stripped of his poet laureateship. All this is far too interesting to have anything to do with John Locke, but it serves to illustrate the frequent (and often dangerous) shifts of political fortune that were to take place during his lifetime.

Unlike the great poet, Locke was to regard his principles as something more than a weather vane. Even so, Locke's principles were to undergo several transformations. The first of these took place during his schooldays at Westminster. Locke had been brought up in a staunchly Parliamentarian home, but at school he found himself making friends with a number of Royalists among the pupils. These encounters, as well as his dislike of Parliamentarian excesses (such as the execution of the king), led him to a more sympathetic view of the Royalists. Learning from experience and toleration—two qualities for which Locke was to become renowned—were already apparent.

Yet in other ways Locke was a slow starter.

He may have been bright at school, but he showed no signs of intellectual giantism. Indeed, he didn't leave Westminster until he was twenty (the age at which his contemporary Gottfried Leibniz was already being offered a professorship). In 1652 Locke enrolled as an undergraduate at Christ Church College, Oxford. Education at Oxford University remained in the medieval era. Undergraduates were required to address their tutors and each other in Latin when in college. The curriculum was limited to the study of the classics, logic, and metaphysics. Despite the new philosophy of Descartes and recent widespread advances in science and mathematics, Aristotle and scholasticism reigned supreme. Undergraduates had the worst of both worlds, for even the time-honored benefits of a medieval education had been abolished. A short while earlier the bordellos and low-life taverns of Oxford had been closed down by the aptly titled vice-chancellor of the university.

The menu of nonstop classics and scholasticism was so boring that even Locke was driven to seek intellectual nourishment elsewhere. He began taking an interest in chemical experiments and medicine. Experimental science had recently been introduced to Oxford by John Wilkins, but it remained a fringe interest. It was viewed with much the same intellectual disdain as present-day universities tend to regard ESP or economics, and its introduction to Oxford had long been opposed. (The fact that Wilkins was Cromwell's brother-in-law may well have helped in overcoming this opposition.)

Locke was introduced to medicine by his former schoolfriend Richard Lower. Medical knowledge was still largely based on Aristotle and the ancient Greek authorities, such as Galen and Hippocrates; but some felt the need to extend this knowledge by scientific investigation and experiment. These had already led to great advances in the study of anatomy—such as William Harvey's discovery of the circulation of the blood. (As a result of this, Locke's friend Lower undertook a daring experiment—daring for his patient as much as for himself—and became the first man to perform a successful blood transfusion.) Even so, for practical purposes medicine remained largely at the sawbones and leeches stage. Locke read avidly of the latest developments but refrained from taking up medical carpentry as a hobby.

By the late 1650s the Commonwealth was being run by the Puritan element, and the country was beginning to suffer from the postrevolutionary religious fanaticism that has now become the norm, even after atheist revolutions. The English have always been very good at being boring, and several times in their history have emerged for considerable periods as undisputed world masters in the field. This was one of them. Under the Puritans all conspicuous signs of enjoyment were rigorously banned. Even Christmas was banned, despite what it celebrated. Citizens were expected to work all day and spend the rest of their time conforming. Life was given over to Puritan indoctrination, the thought police, informers (on the likes of wicked Christmas pudding eaters), and long sessions spent studying the principles of Markism, Lukism, and Johnism. Until in the end even the English had had enough, and decided to invite Charles II to take over. They preferred to be ruled by a drunk-ard who lived with a prostitute, rather than do without Christmas pudding.

Meanwhile Locke's father had fallen seri-ously ill. Locke learned that he was being treated by the celebrated Irish doctor Edmund Meara, and wrote to his father expressing his confidence that he was in safe hands and would soon re-cover. This is curious as Dr. Meara was already notorious for having denounced Harvey's dis-covery of the circulation of the blood as a hoax, and had written a virulent pamphlet attacking Locke's pioneering medical friend Lower. As a result of Dr. Meara's attentions, Locke's father soon got worse, and within a few months he was dead. Although Locke did travel to Somerset be-fore the end (and even called in a new doctor), his behavior here remains inexplicable. Could he have harbored some (perhaps unconscious) re-sentment against his father? Locke's father had been strict at home but could well have lost au-thority when he was temporarily ruined by the civil war. In later life Locke always referred to his father respectfully, but as it was his habit to keep his deeper feelings to himself we can only speculate.

As a result of his father's death Locke inherited a parcel of land and some cottages. The rent from these provided him with an income on which he could have lived modestly for the rest of his life. But Locke had no wish to become a gentleman. By now he had graduated and become a don at Christ Church. The Restoration had brought with it a new libertarianism, and Locke took advantage of this—in his own prudent fashion. He began casting his eyes around at the ladies (who wished to be known as such in those days, and usually behaved like them—except at the royal court and in Restoration comedies).

To judge from the portraits we have of Locke, he was an oddly handsome man, in a rather austere, distinguished manner. This may have been offset by his constant poor health. He appears to have suffered from asthma since childhood. Some have attributed this to psychosomatic causes, and indeed there may have been tensions in his childhood home. A good-looking mother of lower social standing married to an unambitious, sometimes impecunious man ten years her senior, who spent long periods away fighting in the civil war, hardly seems a recipe for domestic bliss. But asthma didn't stop John Locke's roving eye. Unfortunately Locke had been brought up in a Parliamentary household that espoused Puritan ways. Although he had by now transferred his sympathies to the Royalists, he never fully abandoned his former allegiance. At heart, something of the Puritan ethic remained—both in his behavior and in his choice of ladies. He would write them long, amorous letters, and they would reply in equally amorous fashion. I quote from a typical example:

"Worthy Sir,

You are not able to imagine with what content and satisfaction I read over your civil and most obliging letter. . . .

I am sorry to hear that you rode out of your way, and repent with grief that I should be the cause of it, for I assure you that it was my prayers that you might have a happy journey. . . ."

22

And so on, ending: "I remain, your cordial friend. . . ."

Locke replied a week later: "That my returns are not so quick as yours is owing to an impossibility of finding that ecstasy your excellent letter first put me into, for which a week's time is but little to recover myself."

Unsurprisingly, not much came of these often prolonged dalliances, which were sometimes daringly conducted with more than one lady at a time.

But Locke may well have been a little disingenuous about the reasons for his weeklong delay in replying to his cordial friend. Despite his poor health, he set himself a heavy schedule and read long into the night.

Ostensibly Locke may have been a lecturer in ancient Greek, but he nonetheless devoted most of his time to scientific studies. Yet, though he theoretically favored practical experiment, in practice his studies remained purely theoretical.

Science appears to have fulfilled a deep need in Locke. Like his country, he remained divided between the "unreflective adhesion to tradition" of the Royalists and the "enthusiasm" (i.e., un-examined emotional fervor) of the Puritans. Science was Locke's way out of this dilemma. Here was a subject that relied purely upon experience (rather than tradition), and arrived at its truths through experiment (rather than fervent conviction).

Locke's reading of rational science eventually led him to the rational philosophy of Descartes. Here at last, at the late age of thirty-four, he discovered his subject. It was Descartes who gave him "a relish of philosophical studies." The philosophy of Descartes was to have a decisive influence on Locke. Indeed, to this day some French commentators consider him as one of Descartes's followers. But this is ridiculous—as is shown by Voltaire, who rejected Descartes but was heavily influenced by Locke.

Locke certainly appreciated Descartes's importance in overthrowing Aristotle and putting an end to centuries of stifling Scholasticism. He also admired Descartes's method. In order to arrive at an indisputable bedrock of truth, Descartes doubted the evidence of his senses and even the workings of his mind. Knowledge gained from such sources could never be absolutely certain—we can be deluded by both our senses and the workings of our mind. How can we know for certain that we are not dreaming, or that what we are seeing is not a mirage? When we reach a mathematical answer, it is always possible that we have made a mistake in our previous calculations. Having cast doubt on everything, Descartes arrived at his famous conclusion: "Cogito ergo sum" (I think, therefore I am). This alone was certain. On this foundation he then reconstructed a surer world by means of reason and deduction. Locke accepted that Descartes's method did away with many accepted notions and preconceptions, but his instincts were scientific. He mistrusted Descartes's reasoning and deduction as a method of arriving at the truth about the world. In Locke's view this could only be discovered by induction: *scientific* method.

Locke was encouraged in this view by the French thinker Pierre Gassendi, one of Descartes's most penetrating critics. Gassendi was a mathematician of some brilliance, but it was in his life that he managed to square the circle. Gassendi succeeded in combining the roles of priest, philosopher, and scientist. As a philosopher he espoused Epicureanism (which didn't believe in a life after death), and as a scientist he was the first to observe the planetary transit of Mercury around the sun (when the pope still decreed that the sun and the planets circled the earth). In his capacity as a Catholic priest, one can only wonder how Gassendi managed to reduce this circular thinking to the square of Catholic orthodoxy.

Gassendi insisted that all knowledge was based on sensory perception. This was as vital for Locke as the *cogito* was for Descartes: it was to be the foundation on which Locke built his philosophy.

Locke never acknowledged his debt to Gassendi. This is very much in character. Throughout his life Locke remained an inordinately secretive man. In his notebooks he used a coded form of shorthand as well as various inscrutable ciphers. When he received letters he was in the habit of deleting or excising altogether names and places. Even when writing to his women friends he sometimes used invisible ink in his more suggestive passages—though it must be stressed that "suggestive" is very much a relative term where Locke is concerned. ("If the opinion which tells us that everyone has his tutelar angel is true, I am confident that you are mine, seeing that I find that under the protection of your company I am not only the happier but the better, too; and that those evils which assault me in other places dare not approach me while I am near you," is alas as risqué as he gets, invisible ink or no.)

Locke may have attempted to hide his debt to Gassendi, but this secretiveness also led him to deny altogether another cardinal influence on his thought. While still an undergraduate Locke had read Thomas Hobbes's authoritarian political masterpiece, *The Leviathan*. In this Hobbes put forward the pessimistic view that without government "the life of man [is] solitary, poor, nasty, brutish and short." Human beings had found this state of nature unbearable and had congregated in governed societies to overcome it. Any form of government was better than none, and thus we should obey whoever is in charge.

Locke had found himself agreeing with this. "The magistrate of every nation, what way so ever created, *must necessarily have an absolute and arbitrary power over all the indifferent actions of his people.*" This was an understandable view during the troubled years following the civil war, in the midst of "this great bedlam of England." Yet it is a far cry from the toleration that was to be the cornerstone of Locke's later philosophy. Over the years Locke's ideas gradually evolved away from this early view, but he always denied that it was Hobbes who had first influenced him and inspired him to think about political philosophy.

By the time Locke had become a don at Christ Church, his thoughts on political philosophy had begun to deepen. In 1663 he wrote, but didn't publish, a paper entitled the *Law of Nature.* This marks a decisive stage in Locke's thought, boldly linking philosophy and politics—in a way that had not been done before and has seldom been usefully improved upon since. Locke suggested that the vital element in all political problems is the nature of human beings, and that to understand this nature we must first discover how human beings arrive at their knowledge of the world they inhabit. Later attempts to ignore this profound link between philosophy and politics have usually resulted in either inhuman philosophy or inhuman politics. As we shall see, these problems lead directly to Locke's later philosophy and to his more optimistic view of man's basic nature.

After four years of dalliance with Oxford ladies and teaching ancient Greek, Locke decided to strike out for fresh pastures. In 1665 he secured an appointment as secretary on a diplomatic mission to Brandenburg. Judging from his letters home he didn't much like the foreign grub, which was "more a mess than a meal"; and on one occasion he was even served "a piece of powdered beef covered with preserved quinces," which was far too Germanic for his tastes. Despite offers of further diplomatic work he returned to his rooms at Oxford. Here he went on reading the latest works by Descartes and pursuing his amateur interest in medicine—taking care to avoid going out too much in case he caught the plague, which was raging through the country at the time.

It was at Oxford that Locke met a rather ugly little aristocrat who was to play a decisive role in his life. Lord Ashley was less than five feet tall but a man of forceful character. He was also a daring and astute politician. He had originally supported the Royalists but switched sides in the middle of the civil war when he suspected that Charles I was planning to sell out to the Catholics. During the Commonwealth Ashley was appointed by Cromwell to the Council of State, but he later fell out with his boss. In 1660 Ashley was one of the party sent by Parliament to tell Charles II to come home, all is forgiven. At the time Locke met him, Ashley was one of the most powerful political figures in the country. Ashley seems to have taken to Locke from the start. Within no time he had appointed the philosopher as his personal physician. Despite the fact that Locke had no qualifications for this job, he successfully delivered Ashley's wife of a child. When Ashley began suffering from a suppurating abscess of the liver, you'd think that Locke might have called in a doctor. But not a bit of it. After consulting a couple of medical treatises he decided to operate. A surgeon-barber was summoned and ordered to slice open his lordship, whereupon Locke inserted a silver tube to drain the abscess. Lord Ashley continued to wear this tube for the rest of his days and was convinced that Locke had saved his life. Amazingly, he almost certainly had.

Besides serving the Ashley family as a quack, Locke also acted as tutor to the children, and even carried out negotiations for the marriage of Lord Ashley's son. Aristocratic English marriages, like those between central European peasants, were invariably arranged with much hard bargaining between the two families involved. For peasants and bluebloods alike, breeding qualities, land, and cash were usually the main considerations—the aesthetic merits and finer feelings of the participants being as little considered as they were evident. After completing the customary horse trading, Locke secured a suitable contract and the marriage went ahead.

Locke was now living in London and was able to meet regularly with his intellectual peers. Here they would discuss the latest philosophical and scientific developments (such as how a man can survive with a silver tube inserted into his abdomen). Locke also wrote another political paper, which would almost certainly have guaranteed him a lifetime behind bars in any other country except Holland. In this paper he asserted that no one knows enough to dictate to another the form of his religion; that to compel an individual against his will achieves only lip-service conformity; and that we are all responsible to God, which not only makes us moral beings but also presupposes our freedom. The fact that these original views now appear to us as pious commonplaces reflects on Locke's wisdom rather than our judgment.

In 1672 Ashley was made Lord Shaftesbury and appointed lord chancellor, which was then the highest political post in the land. Lord Shaftesbury (as he is usually known in the history books) had always looked upon Locke as more than just his personal physician-cum-matchmaker. He frequently sought Locke's advice on political and intellectual matters. (In those far-off days these two elements were not mutually exclusive.) Shaftesbury and Locke held much in common, especially their attitude toward the benefits of foreign trade and their views on toleration. (Though in Shaftesbury's case the latter had a considerable lacuna. He didn't believe in tolerance toward Catholics, and is recalled by one historian as "one of the most passionate anti-Catholics in English history.")

Shaftesbury now had the good judgment to appoint Locke to various posts in the administration, and for a couple of years Locke became secretary to the newly formed Council of Trade and Plantations. As a result Locke was able to put his political theories into practice when he helped to draft the constitution for the new American colony of Carolina.

Locke's ideas on liberal democracy were to have a more lasting effect on political philosophy than any others in the history of this notorious so-called science. It is the anti-heroes such as Machiavelli, Louis XIV ("I am the state"), and Marx who grab the limelight. Yet it is Locke whose ideas are embodied in the United States Constitution, the British constitution (as well as the constitutions of its former colonies through-out the globe), and even for a brief period the French constitution.

Locke continued to discuss his ideas with his intellectual cronies, and after one particularly disputatious evening with "five or six friends meeting at my chambers," he decided to try to set down his philosophical ideas in coherent form. These were eventually to constitute the basis of his masterwork, *An Essay Concerning Human Understanding*. (When I was recently looking through the first edition of this work in the British Museum, I came across a note in the margin. This was written in a shaky hand in fad-ing sepia ink, apparently by Locke's friend Tyrrell. It referred to that original meeting in Locke's chambers: "This was in the winter of 1673 as I remember myself being one of those.") That historic evening could be said to have marked the start of empiricism—the first philosophy since the origin of the subject more than two thousand years earlier to take the radical step of basing itself on common sense.

From now on, for the next twenty years, the problem of human knowledge, how we come by it, and what precisely it is, was to remain Locke's major concern. But by 1675 Locke's asthma had deteriorated to the extent that he could no longer continue living in London. The air, heavy with coal dust, smoke, and fogs, plagued his lungs. Long fits of coughing and wheezing often reduced him to a state of exhaustion. Locke was forced to give up most of his administrative work and retire to Oxford, where he was still nominally a don at Christ Church. Around the same time Lord Shaftesbury fell from favor with the king and was dismissed. Locke then left for France, allegedly on account of his health, but almost certainly to carry out some politicking for Shaftesbury as well. He was to remain in France for four years. Here he came into contact with the Gassendists (followers of the scientist-priest Gassendi, who had died twenty years earlier).

They advocated the experimental approach adopted by Kepler and Galileo, believing in a science based on atomic particles. Like their master, they rejected both Scholasticism and Descartes in favor of an empirical and hedonistic approach (though the latter may appear sadly theoretical to modern sensibilities). The idea that we learn through experience, and the principle that in social philosophy pleasure must be seen as good, were to play a major role in Locke's thinking.

During this period Locke appears to have acted on occasion as a tutor to the sons of English aristocrats and to have traveled extensively throughout France. His health continued to bother him. Drawing on his extensive medical researches, he eventually diagnosed himself as suffering from phthisis, which causes wasting of the body, especially the lungs. The health resort of Montpellier was renowned for curing phthisis, and at one stage Locke traveled there to take the cure. But this was of little avail, not least because of Locke's mistaken self-diagnosis. On his travels he continued to complain about the food. At one inn "the whole bill of fare" was "nothing but cabbage and a frog that was caught in it and some haws [hawthorn fruit] of last season." He didn't take to the French much, either (men all had the pox, Jesuits sleeping with the nuns, etc.).

While Locke was traveling on the newly opened Canal du Midi between Toulouse and Agen, he had an accident—"a great pole having fallen on my head in the boat." But he had recovered by the time he arrived back in Paris, where he saw Louis XIV and his queen at the opera. He also had another chance to put his (still unqualified) medical skills to practice. The British ambassador's wife had become delirious with agony as a result of a toothache. Her (qualified) French physician had already pulled out two perfectly good teeth to no avail. Locke examined the patient and diagnosed trigeminal neuralgia—apparently the first diagnosis of its kind in medical history. He prescribed a violent purge, which astonishingly did the trick. (As a cure for toothache, was this too a first? One wonders.)

When Locke returned to England in 1679 the country was in the grip of a political crisis.

Charles II was intent on making his Catholic brother James heir to the throne, and Shaftesbury was leading the parliamentary opposition to this move. Shaftesbury had already been locked up in the Tower for this trouble but was now back in favor with the king. He had been appointed lord president of the Privy Council and was attempting to effect a reconciliation between Charles and Parliament. In the midst of all this Locke sent Shaftesbury a paper entitled *Observations on the Growth and Culture of Vines and Olives,* with the aim of "demonstrating that it is possible for something good to come out of France." Unfortunately Shaftesbury had little time to study this fascinating document as he was arrested on a charge of treason, through the machinations of his enemies. (Among these was Locke's old school friend Dryden, who immortalized Shaftesbury in his *Absalom and Achitophel,* which was not only the finest satirical poem to appear in seventeenth century but also one of the most wrongheaded.)

Locke was now almost fifty years old but still had an eye for the ladies—and an active pen too, judging from his correspondence. Although this eye and pen are in no way to be taken as symbolic or euphemistic: Locke just wasn't that sort of person. His intentions appear to have been neither dishonorable nor even honorable—indeed, one is often led to wonder whether he had any intentions at all. In one of his letters he refers to "marriage or death (which are so very nearly the same thing)." Then in 1682 he met Damaris Cudworth, the twenty-four-year-old daughter of a Cambridge Platonist. Damaris was by far the most intelligent woman Locke had ever met. She could converse with him on equal terms. She was "prone to outbursts" (as was Locke, on rare occasions) but was also possessed of emotional understanding. She appears to have fallen in love with Locke right from the start. He had retained his distinguished good looks, though his illness left him gaunt and rather frail. But Locke was interested only in his usual type of friendship—a sort of Chinese water torture by correspondence. They wrote poems to each other and exchanged letters, calling each other Philoclea and Philander (an odd choice, under the circumstances). Philo-

clea claimed that she was descended from Cad-
wallader, the legendary last king of the ancient
Britons, and Locke referred to her as his "gov-
erness" (once again, no impropriety whatsoever
should be assumed here). Then Philoclea fell out
of love and decided that all she too wanted was
friendship—whereupon, in the usual Restoration
farce of the emotions, Locke found that he was
now in love with her.

Meanwhile Shaftesbury was tried in London
but acquitted by a sympathetic jury. He at once
fled for his life to Holland. (He was to die there
a year later of "gout of the stomach," a diagnosis worthy of Locke himself.) In England, anyone
associated with Shaftesbury was now under sus-
picion. Locke too was in danger. At Oxford he
realized that he was under surveillance by spies.
According to a report from one spy: "John Locke
lives a very cunning unintelligible life." At last a
lifetime of secretiveness came into its own. The
professional spies proved no match for the wily
philosopher, and Locke soon gave them the slip,
making his way to Holland. But only just in
time. The king immediately stripped Locke of his

post at Christ Church, placed him on a list of eighty-four traitors, and despatched an extradition order to the Dutch government. Locke was forced to go into hiding in The Hague.

During this period Locke learned that Damaris Cudworth had married a north-country widower called Sir Francis Masham. It's difficult to gauge Locke's precise feelings at this point. He loved Damaris, as he probably hadn't loved any other woman in his life. Yet he may have reasoned that he was too ill, too old, and too set in his scholarly ways to make much of a husband to a woman less than half his age. But as Locke realized in his philosophy: we don't learn from reason, we learn from experience. He had never had this experience before, and my guess is that it probably hurt him deeply at the time, though he didn't show it.

In 1685 Charles II died and his Catholic brother James II ascended to the throne, confirming Shaftesbury's worst fears. Meanwhile Locke concentrated his energies on his philosophy. By now he was putting the finishing touches to *An Essay Concerning Human Understanding*.

This opens with a delightful Epistle to the Reader, which describes the work as "the diversion of some of my idle and heavy hours: if it has the good luck to prove so of any of thine, and thou hast half so much Pleasure in reading, as I had in writing it, thou wilt as little think thy Money as I do my Pains ill bestowed." The philosophy it contained was just as sympathetic and as far-reaching as any since Descartes. It was not as profoundly original as Descartes's work, nor as brilliant; but by dethroning reason in favor of experience it appeared to later philosophers to be closer to the truth. Without Descartes there might have been no modern philosophy. But it was Locke who fathered its main line of development—the British empiricists, who then provoked Kant to produce the greatest philosophical system of them all, which in turn gave rise to the elephantine folly of Hegel, and the consequent disbelief in all systems by anyone except Marxists and optimistic punters.

According to Locke we have no such thing as intuitive ideas about Right and Wrong, God, etc. Despite this, Locke firmly believed in God.

Descartes may have had his secret doubts on occasion; Spinoza avoided the issue by turning everything into God; and Leibniz probably didn't believe in God, though he pretended to. But Locke was unwavering in his belief, despite the fact that there isn't really any room for God in his philosophy. "There is nothing in the mind except what was first in the senses." We begin with a *tabula rasa* (blank sheet). Human knowledge is derived from outer experience, and reflection (Locke's word for introspection), which enables us to discover what goes on in our minds. We use reason to draw conclusions from these experiences. In this way we arrive at generalizations, laws, and the truths of mathematics.

Like Descartes, Locke believed that the empirical knowledge we gain from the senses can only be probable. But unlike Descartes, Locke didn't let this undermine all such knowledge. Instead of retreating into reason, he used common sense. Empirical knowledge and the knowledge we derive from it may only be probable, but by the use of intuition and deduction we can assess *how* probable. (This division between reason

43

and common sense, which first appeared with Descartes and Locke, was to become a permanent feature of Anglo-French philosophical relations. Today it has developed to the point where the French very reasonably regard English philosophy as nothing whatsoever to do with philosophy, and English common sense confronted with French philosophy has come to an identical conclusion.)

In Book II of his *Essay Concerning Human Understanding,* Locke explains that there are two distinct types of ideas that make up our empirical knowledge of the world. Simple ideas, such as color, heat and cold, and taste are indivisible. Complex ideas, on the other hand, are made up of combinations of these ideas. Such combinations may result in things that have no corresponding entity in the real world—such as ghosts or UFOs.

Locke also distinguishes between the primary and secondary qualities of objects. (Here he drew heavily on the notions of Galileo and the Gassendists.) Primary qualities are those possessed by all objects, regardless of what they are.

44

These include such qualities as extension, solidity, and mobility. The ideas produced in us by our perception of these qualities closely resemble the qualities themselves. In secondary qualities, such as taste, color, and smell, this is not the case. The taste and smell of a bad egg are merely powers in this objectionable object that produce ideas that do not resemble their cause.

Locke's thinking on these matters reflects the revolution that was taking place in the science of the period. It is no accident that Locke was a contemporary of great scientific thinkers ranging from Galileo to Newton. And the scientific revolution was firmly rooted in physics—the "real" properties of objects, those that could be measured—rather than ephemeral and less quantifiable qualities such as color and smell. These "real" measurable qualities appear in Locke's philosophy as the primary qualities of extension, solidity, and mobility (which in physics are calculated as volume, weight, and speed).

In Book IV Locke distinguishes between the various kinds of knowledge that we gain from our ideas. He defines knowledge itself as "the perception of the connection and agreement or disagreement . . . of any of our ideas." We perceive relations between our ideas by means of reason. This perception can be direct, in which case it gives rise to "intuitive knowledge." For instance, we perceive directly that the color red is not the color green, or that a triangle is not a square.

Our perception can also connect ideas in an indirect manner, and this gives rise to "demonstrative knowledge." This particularly applies to the knowledge of mathematics. For instance, we do not perceive directly that the three angles of a triangle add up to 180 degrees. We connect these two ideas by means of mathematical reasoning.

The third type of knowledge is more immediate. This is the "sensitive knowledge" we have of things outside ourselves that directly correspond to our ideas of them. When we see a friend on a daily basis we have a direct sensitive knowledge of this person. This is very different from the similar mental picture we form of him if we remember him when he is not present. This memory may be faulty or open to doubt, where the direct experience is not. Sensitive knowledge may be less certain than intuitive or demonstrative knowledge, but it is not open to serious doubt. Owing to the consistency and repetitiveness of such experiences, we can safely assume that such external things correspond precisely with the ideas we have of them. This is a big assumption, which appears to be in line with "common sense." But on closer examination it skates on thin ice over a multitude of philosophical problems. (How can we possibly know that a rock in fact concurs with our perception of it, when this perception results from organs that have nothing to do with that rock? In what sense does the rock resemble the reactions of my retina, the sensations of the nerves in my fingers?) These were difficulties that lay ahead, difficulties that beset any new vision of the world. The vision itself was what mattered. Such empiricism dealt the ancient ideas of the Scholastics a blow from which they would never recover.

Locke had rejected the Aristotelean notion whereby the words with which we classify things correspond to the "real essence" of things. According to this, the word *apple* corresponded to the "substantial form" that was embodied in all apples. For Locke, essences were replaced by ideas. But this was no sleight-of-hand substitution; it represented a profound shift in the way we see the world. Instead of being something within the object, like its essence, the idea was a purely mental construct. After perceiving many apples, we come up with the word *apple* as a useful classification. Such ideas "belong not to the real existence of things; but are the inventions and creatures of the understanding, made by it for its own use." Experience is the basis of our knowledge, and it is processed by the mind in a scientific fashion. The knowledge thus gained is useful, practical—rather than a thing corresponding to unseen abstract essences or "substantial forms."

In 1688 the English decided they'd had enough of James II, and the so-called Glorious Revolution took place. The Dutch Protestant William, Prince of Orange, was asked to become king, but only on certain strict conditions—which left effective power in the hands of Parliament. William sailed from Holland, and a few months later his wife, Mary, followed. Locke accompanied Mary, Princess of Orange, and returned to England in the wake of the Glorious Revolution.

Locke was now free to publish *An Essay Concerning Human Understanding,* which he did in 1689 (despite the date 1690 that appears on the frontispiece). In direct contravention of Locke's wish to clear away "some of the rubbish that lies in the way of knowledge," his work soon began attracting the usual barrage of criticism, notably from Leibniz. In the hope of forestalling more rubbish, Locke quickly began making heavy alterations in his copy of the book, rebutting each of these criticisms as they appeared, before further editions were published. (This philosophy on the hoof can be observed in the British Museum's first edition, which has long emendations in Locke's own hand.)

1698 also saw the publication of Locke's other great work, his *Two Treatises of Government.* He had initially written this in 1681, but the times had been far too dangerous for the publication of such a liberal political work. He had rewritten parts of this manuscript during his enforced stay in Holland, and made further alterations, taking into account his approval of the Glorious Revolution, when he returned to England. This caused several critics to accuse him of writing the work simply to justify the revolution. This was not the case. In his work he justifies revolution, but he had not written it to justify the Glorious Revolution—more to prepare the way for it.

Others accused Locke of writing this work in the hope of receiving a post from the new king. Nothing could have been farther from the truth. Locke in fact even turned down a job from William. When he was offered the post of British ambassador to the court of Frederick III of Brandenburg, he politely declined. An ambassador needed to socialize, and Locke declared that he wasn't up to the "warm drinking" habits of the Germans. William would be better off sending an ambassador who was willing to "drink his share" instead of "the soberest man in England."

The first of Locke's *Two Treatises of Government* is a refutation of the ideas of Robert Filmer, a highly popular political theorist of the period, whose fame died long before his audience. (Locke's secretive practices had ensured that he was spared such fickleness.) Filmer was a neo-Hobbesian who believed in the Divine Right of Kings. Locke had long since suppressed his Hobbesian ideas (along with *almost* all manuscript evidence of them), and this was his attempt to present a viable alternative.

In the second treatise Locke attempts to discover the roots of government. In the original state of nature, he argues, people were free and equal. But such freedom and equality were largely theoretical. People were simply unable to get along together without infringing on one another's rights. Locke believed that the law of nature grants us each natural rights. We have a right to life and a right to liberty, as long as this doesn't infringe on the liberty and natural rights of others. But without an element of coercion we are unable to enjoy these natural rights. To do so we must join together in a social contract. This guarantees our natural rights by establishing a government that enforces laws to protect them. A framework of security is established. Under this condition, our theoretical liberty may be restricted but our actual liberty is enhanced.

The consent of the people is the sole basis for this government's authority. Locke makes this perfectly clear: "whosoever in authority exceeds the power given him by the law, and makes use of the force he has under his command to compass that upon the subject which the law allows not . . . may be opposed as any other man, who by force invades the right of another." If the government, or ruler, violates the rights of individual citizens, then the people have the right to revolt and get rid of this ruler or government. "To take away and destroy the property of the people, or to reduce them to slavery [puts a ruler] into a state of war with the people, who are thereupon absolved from any further obedience, and are left to the common refuge, which God hath provided for all men against force and violence." In other words, revolution.

Locke believed that government should act solely for the purpose for which it was originally formed—namely, the protection of life, liberty, and property. "When any number of men have so consented to make one community or government, they are thereby presently incorporated and make one body politic, wherein the majority have a right to act and conclude the rest." This laid the foundation upon which modern liberal democracy was built. These were the ideas that a century later inspired the American Declaration of Independence and the French Revolution. Such sentiments may sound simplistic in the modern era of populous technological democracies, but they remain very much the beliefs and principles of the citizens who inhabit them.

Although Locke's lady-friend had now married and become Lady Masham, he still kept in touch with her. There was obviously a deep rapport between the philosopher and his understanding intellectual correspondent. But she only partly accepted Locke's empiricism, faithfully retaining an element of her father's Platonism—a combination that would have taxed any but the most accommodating of intellects.

Lady Masham appeared to understand Locke and his emotional needs like no other, and he obviously blossomed in her company. He became a regular visitor to Sir Francis and Lady Masham's country house Oates, located twenty miles northeast of London in Essex. The country air suited him, and after a couple of years the Mashams invited him to make Oates his home.

This is a story with a happy ending. Locke gratefully accepted the Mashams' invitation, moved in, and they all appeared to enjoy themselves. Sir Francis was the local member of Parliament for the county of Essex. He was a typical English gentleman: charming, thick as a brick, and a convinced philistine. He was only too pleased that his intellectual wife had someone to talk with, leaving him free to go to London on parliamentary business. He seems to have embodied all the best qualities of tolerance, such as Locke's philosophy proposed, in his dealings with its author. They had nothing to say to each other, and indeed seemingly talked very little to each other as they went about their separate lives. Whether this was due to mutual respect or indifference is difficult to tell. This was a quintessentially English ménage à trois, without a hint of scandal.

Oates was a modest country house dating from Tudor times. It was built of local red brick, had Gothic battlements, and was encompassed by a moat. It was situated at High Lever, a village deep in the Essex countryside between Harlow and Chipping Ongar. The house had a pleasant rose garden with a lawn beside a pond, where Locke liked to sit and read in the summer. (For some unaccountable reason, the whole place was flattened in 1802 and the site was left derelict. The lawns reverted to water meadows, the pond became clogged with weeds, and much of the moat silted up. The site of the house is now a grassy meadow in open countryside beside a small lake which is home to a sizable colony of ducks and geese. While I was walking across this meadow recently on a cold, grey February morning, I came across a small patch of rubble breaking the surface of the grass. It contained several

fragments of old red brick: all that apparently remained of Oates.)

Locke moved into two rooms on the first
floor off the paneled entrance hall, bringing with
him a few pieces of his own furniture and the
usual bare essentials required by any philosopher
(five thousand books, according to his biogra-
pher). He paid one pound sterling a week for his
keep and that of his servant, and one shilling a
week for the stabling of his horse.

But Locke had not retired. Far from it. He
was now looked upon as the intellectual *émi-
nence grise* of the Whigs, the leading party in
Parliament, and was constantly being consulted
on policy matters. He appears to have traveled to
London frequently but always returned to the
country when his asthma attacks became too
much for him. He even took on a senior post at
the Board of Trade and Plantations.

In the middle of winter in 1698 Locke was
summoned for an urgent meeting with the king
at Kensington Palace. Reluctantly he clambered
into the coach, his chest heavily wrapped in lay-
ers of rugs, and set off on the long drive down

the ice-rutted turnpike across the bleak, snow-covered countryside. For some reason Locke always kept the purpose of this visit to the king a secret, which he wouldn't confide even to Lady Masham. Most sources agree that he was probably offered—and politely refused—the job of ambassador to France, a post that was more than ornamental in those days.

In between his public duties, Locke mixed with the intellectuals of his day. This species, now extinct in Britain, flourished in seventeenth-century London—without any question of there being two cultures. Locke would have met most of the leading literary and scientific figures of his time, not including, one hopes, his old schoolmate the dreadful Dryden, who was by now reduced to the ignominious task of translating Virgil, a fate he thoroughly deserved. Locke became particularly friendly with Isaac Newton, who often came to visit him at Oates. Those who wonder what the two greatest minds of their time discussed while sitting in the garden watching gravity at work in the orchard, will be disappointed. Newton tried to explain gravity to

Locke, but the philosopher had to pretend to understand—the only example of intellectual deceit by Locke that I have so far come across. Instead, the Laurel and Hardy of contemporary learning (now look what a fine mess they've got us into) spent their time discussing the Epistles of St. Paul. These were a great favorite with Newton, who devoted much of his energy to writing commentaries on the Bible. He remained convinced to his dying day that this was his real life's work, for which he would be remembered in the years to come long after gravity had been forgotten.

In 1699 Locke was finally forced to resign from his post at the Board of Trade and Plantations. He was now sixty-seven, and his asthma was gradually worsening. He was to live for another four years at Oates, industriously writing on such diverse matters as religious tolerance, the size of the groat (the smallest coin of the realm), and the effect of interest rates on the likes of Sir Francis. On October 28, 1704, he died, having spent the previous night with his frail, wheezing frame supported in the arms of Lady Masham.

Locke was buried at High Lever Church, where you can still see his red-brick tomb today, behind some railings against the flintstone south wall. After he died Lady Masham abandoned her husband at Oates and went to live in Bath—giving rise to speculation that her attachment to Locke may have been more than platonic. Either way, all three of them are now buried at High Lever Church, Lady Masham lying dutifully beside her husband in the nave.

Afterword

Locke's life spanned the era from Galileo to Newton. It is no coincidence that during his lifetime heliocentricity became accepted, calculus and celestial gravity were discovered, the circulation of the blood was detected, and chemistry began to free itself from alchemy and establish itself as a genuine science. Such accomplishments were literally unthinkable in terms of Aristotle and Scholasticism. (For instance, Scholasticism rigidly clung to the ancient Greek notion that everything was composed of an admixture of earth, air, fire, and water. Only after the Irish chemist Robert Boyle had rejected this theory of the four elements in *The Sceptical Chymist* could chemistry base itself upon a study of the actual elements and the way they combined to form compounds.)

The emerging modern world was completely different from the one that was lived in by the medievalists. This new world needed a new way of thinking, and in philosophy this was provided by Locke. His *Essay Concerning Human Understanding* was to be the most influential philosophical work throughout Europe for the next hundred years.

It is also no coincidence that Locke witnessed the last civil war in England and the first successful revolution in modern Europe. His political thought laid the foundations for liberal democracy. But these two elements in Locke's thinking—the political and the purely philosophical—were not only linked in Locke's understanding, but also by profound historical changes that were taking place. Luther had liberated people from the authority of the church, allowing them private judgment and a personal conscience. In the same way, Locke delivered them from Aristotelianism's "thralldom of error and prejudice" by appealing directly to experience. What was happening in Europe was nothing less than the emergence of the individual. This new evolutionary freak—widespread individuality—sought to express itself. Locke's philosophy showed it the way. On the one hand liberty of thought, on the other liberty of action. The two went hand in hand: in life as well as in the works of Locke. This was his gift to the world. And no matter how succeeding generations of critics may have picked holes in his philosophy or rendered it outmoded, this gift will remain forever undeniable.

From Locke's Writings

He who has raised himself above the alms-basket, and, not content to live lazily on scraps of begged opinions, sets his own thoughts on work, to find and follow truth, will (whatever he lights on) not miss the hunter's satisfaction; every moment of his pursuit will reward his pains with some delight; and he will have reason to think his time not ill spent, even when he cannot much boast of any great acquisition.

—*An Essay Concerning Human Understanding: Epistle to the Reader*

There are [no innate principles] to which all mankind give an universal consent. I shall begin with the speculative, and instance in those magnified principles of demonstration, *Whatsoever is, is* and *It is impossible for the same thing to be and not to be,* which of all others I think have the most allowed title to innate. These have so settled a reputation of maxims universally received that it will, no doubt, be thought strange if anyone should seem to question it. But yet I take the liberty to say that these propositions are so far from having an universal assent, that there are a great part of mankind to whom they are not so much as known.

For, first, it is evident that all *children* and *idiots* have not the least apprehension or thought of them.

—*An Essay Concerning Human Understanding,*
Bk 1, Ch 2

Let us then suppose that the mind be, as we say, white paper void of all characters, without any *ideas.* How comes it to be furnished? Whence comes it by that vast store which the busy and boundless fancy of man has painted on it with an almost endless variety? Whence has it all the materials of reason and knowledge? To this I answer, in one word, from *experience;* in that all our knowledge is founded, and from that it ultimately derives itself.

—*An Essay Concerning Human Understanding,*
Bk 2, Ch 1

Our observation, employed either about *external sensible objects, or about the internal operations of our minds perceived and reflected on by ourselves, is that which supplies our understanding with all the materials of thinking.* These two are the fountains of knowledge, from whence all the *ideas* we have, or can naturally have, do spring.

—*An Essay Concerning Human Understanding,*
Bk 2, Ch 1

The power to produce any *idea* in our mind, I call *quality* of the subject wherein that power is. Thus a snowball having the power to produce in us the *ideas of white, cold,* and *round,* the powers to produce those ideas in us, as they are in the snowball, I call *qualities*; and as they are sensations, or perceptions, in our understanding, I call them *ideas.*

—*An Essay Concerning Human Understanding,*
Bk 2, Ch 8

Such *qualities* which in truth are nothing in the objects themselves but powers to produce various sensations in us by their *primary qualities,* i.e. by the bulk, figure, texture, and motion of their insensible parts, as colors, sounds, tastes, etc. These I call *secondary qualities.* . . . For the power in fire to produce a new color, or consistency in wax or clay, by its primary qualities, is as much a quality in fire as the power it has to produce in me a new *idea* or sensation of warmth or burning, which I felt not before, by the same primary qualities, *viz* the bulk, texture, and motion of its insensible parts.

—*An Essay Concerning Human Understanding,*
Bk 2, Ch 8

The ideas of *primary qualities* of bodies, *are resemblances* of them, and their patterns do really exist in the bodies themselves; but the *ideas* produced in us by these *secondary qualities have no resemblance* of them at all. There is nothing like our *ideas*, existing in the bodies themselves.

—*An Essay Concerning Human Understanding,*
Bk 2, Ch 8

As simple ideas are observed to exist in various combinations united together; so the mind has a power to consider several of them united together, as one *idea*; and that not only are they united in external objects, but as itself has joined them. *Ideas* thus made up of several simple ones put together, I call *complex*, such as are *beauty, gratitude, a man, an army, the universe*; which,

though complicated of various simple *ideas*, or *complex ideas* made up of simple ones, yet are, when the mind pleases, considered each by itself as one entire thing, and signified by one name.
—*An Essay Concerning Human Understanding*,
Bk 2, Ch 12

We can have no *idea* of the place of the universe, though we can of all the parts in it; because beyond that, we have not the *idea* of any fixed, distinct, particular beings, in reference to which, we can imagine it to have any relation of distance, but all beyond it is one uniform space or expansion, wherein the mind finds no variety, no marks.
—*An Essay Concerning Human Understanding*,
Bk 2, Ch 13

Some of our *ideas* have a natural correspondence and connexion one with another; it is the office and excellence of our reason to trace these, and hold them together in that union and correspondence which is founded in their peculiar beings. Besides this, there is another connexion of *ideas* wholly owing to chance or custom; *ideas* that in themselves are not at all of kin, come to be so united in some men's minds that it is very hard to separate them, they always keep in company, and the one no sooner at any time comes into the understanding but its associate appears with it. . . . That there are such associations of them made by custom in the minds of most men, I think nobody will question who has well considered himself or others; and to this, perhaps, might be justly attributed most of the sympathies and antipathies observable in men, which work as strongly and produce as regular effects as if they were natural; and are therefore called so, though they at first had no other original but the accidental connexion of two *ideas*.

—*An Essay Concerning Human Understanding,*
Bk 2, Ch 33

Political power then I take to be *a right* of making laws with penalties of death, and consequently all less penalties, for the regulating and preserving of property, and of employing the force of the community, in the execution of such laws, and in the defense of the commonwealth from foreign injury, and all this only for the public good.

—*Two Treatises of Government*, 2nd, Ch 1

To understand political power right, and derive it from its original, we must consider what state all men are naturally in, and that is, a *state of perfect freedom* to order their actions, and dispose of their possessions, and person as they think fit, within the bounds of the law of nature, without asking leave, or depending upon the will of any other man.

A *state* also of *equality,* wherein all the power and jurisdiction is reciprocal, no one having more than another. . . .

—*Two Treatises of Government*, 2nd, Ch 2

The *state of nature* has a law of nature to govern it, which obliges everyone: and reason, which is that law, teaches all mankind, who will but consult it, that being all equal and independent, no one ought to harm another in his life, health, liberty, or possessions.

—*Two Treatises of Government*, 2nd, Ch 2

Civil government is the proper remedy for the inconveniences of the state of nature, which must certainly be great, where men may be judges in their own case, since 'tis easily to be imagined, that he who was so unjust as to do his brother an injury, will scarce be so just as to condemn himself for it.

—*Two Treatises of Government*, 2nd, Ch 2

'Tis often asked as a mighty objection, *Where are,* or ever were, there any *men in such a state of nature*? To which it may suffice as an answer at present; that since all *princes* and rulers of *independent* governments all through the world, are in a state of nature, 'tis plain the world never was, nor ever will be, without numbers of men in that state.

—*Two Treatises of Government*, 2nd, Ch 2

The *natural liberty* of man is to be free from any superior power on earth, and not to be under the will or legislative authority of man, but to have only the law of nature for his rule. The liberty of man, in society, is to be under no other legislative power but that established, by consent, in the commonwealth, nor under the dominion of any will, or restraint of any law, but what the legislative will enact, according to the trust put in it.

—*Two Treatises of Government*, 2nd, Ch 4

Chronology of Significant Philosophical Dates

6th C B.C.   The beginning of Western philosophy with Thales of Miletus.

End of
6th C B.C.   Death of Pythagoras.

399 B.C.   Socrates sentenced to death in Athens.

c 387 B.C.   Plato founds the Academy in Athens, the first university.

335 B.C.   Aristotle founds the Lyceum in Athens, rival school to the Academy.

324 A.D.   Emperor Constantine moves capital
                  of Roman Empire to Byzantium.

400 A.D.   St. Augustine writes his
                  Confessions. Philosophy absorbed
                  into Christian theology.

410 A.D.   Sack of Rome by Visigoths heralds
                  opening of Dark Ages.

529 A.D.   Closure of Academy in Athens by
                  Emperor Justinian marks end of
                  Hellenic thought.

Mid-13th C   Thomas Aquinas writes his
                  commentaries on Aristotle. Era of
                  Scholasticism.

1453   Fall of Byzantium to Turks, end of
                  Byzantine Empire.

1492   Columbus reaches America.
                  Renaissance in Florence and revival
                  of interest in Greek learning.

1543   Copernicus publishes *On the
                  Revolution of the Celestial Orbs*
                  proving mathematically that the
                  earth revolves around the sun.

1633	Galileo forced by church to recant heliocentric theory of the universe.
1641	Descartes publishes his *Meditations*, the start of modern philosophy.
1677	Death of Spinoza allows publication of his *Ethics*.
1687	Newton publishes *Principia*, introducing concept of gravity.
1689	Locke publishes *Essay Concerning Human Understanding*. Start of empiricism.
1710	Berkeley publishes *Principles of Human Knowledge*, advancing empiricism to new extremes.
1716	Death of Leibniz.
1739–1740	Hume publishes *Treatise of Human Nature*, taking empiricism to its logical limits.
1781	Kant, awakened from his "dogmatic slumbers" by Hume, publishes *Critique of Pure Reason*.

Great era of German metaphysics
begins.

1807   Hegel publishes *The
            Phenomenology of Mind*, high
            point of German metaphysics.

1818   Schopenhauer publishes *The World
            as Will and Representation*,
            introducing Indian philosophy into
            German metaphysics.

1889   Nietzsche, having declared "God is
            dead," succumbs to madness in
            Turin.

1921   Wittgenstein publishes *Tractatus
            Logico-Philosophicus*, claiming the
            "final solution" to the problems of
            philosophy.

1920s   Vienna Circle propounds Logical
            Positivism.

1927   Heidegger publishes *Being and
            Time*, heralding split between
            analytical and Continental
            philosophy.

1943   Sartre publishes *Being and
            Nothingness*, advancing

Heidegger's thought and instigating existentialism.

1953   Posthumous publication of Wittgenstein's *Philosophical Investigations*. High era of linguistic analysis.

Chronology of Locke's Life

1632	John Locke born in Somerset, England.
1642	Outbreak of civil war; father leaves home to join Parliamentarians.
1647–1652	Educated at Westminster School.
1652	Enrolls as undergraduate at Christ Church, Oxford, where he later becomes a don.
1663	Writes, but does not publish, *Law of Nature*.
1665	Member of diplomatic mission to Brandenburg.

1667	Enters service of Lord Ashley (later Earl of Shaftesbury).
1668	Elected to Royal Society, the first great scientific institution.
1675	Travels to France.
1683	After accession of James II, flees to live in exile in Holland.
1689	Returns to England on accession of William of Orange. Publishes *An Essay Concerning Human Understanding*.
1691	Retires to live with Lord and Lady Masham in Essex.
1704	Dies and is buried at High Lever Church.

Recommended Reading

Vere Chappell, ed., *The Cambridge Companion to Locke* (Cambridge University Press, 1994). A selection of essays covering a wide range of Locke's thought.

John Locke, *An Essay Concerning Human Understanding* (Dutton, 1989). His main work on epistemology, which launched empiricism on the philosophical world.

John Locke, *A Letter Concerning Toleration* (Prometheus Books, 1990). Locke's most accessible moral text, with illuminating commentary.

E. J. Lowe, *Locke on Human Understanding* (Routledge, 1997). Selections analyzing Locke's epistemological thought, with some penetrating criticisms.

David L. Thomas, ed., *Locke on Government* (Routledge, 1995). Essays on most aspects of Locke's political thought.

Index

A NOTE ON THE AUTHOR

Paul Strathern has lectured in philosophy and mathematics and now lives and writes in London. A Somerset Maugham prize winner, he is also the author of books on history and travel as well as five novels. His articles have appeared in a great many publications, including the *Observer* (London) and the *Irish Times*. His own degree in philosophy was earned at Trinity College, Dublin.